Western Meadowlarks

Julie Murray

Abdo Kids Junior
is an Imprint of Abdo Kids
abdobooks.com

STATE BIRDS
Abdo Kids

abdobooks.com

Published by Abdo Kids, a division of ABDO, P.O. Box 398166, Minneapolis, Minnesota 55439. Copyright © 2022 by Abdo Consulting Group, Inc. International copyrights reserved in all countries. No part of this book may be reproduced in any form without written permission from the publisher. Abdo Kids Junior™ is a trademark and logo of Abdo Kids.

Printed in the United States of America, North Mankato, Minnesota.

052021

092021

Photo Credits: Alamy, Animals Animals, iStock, Shutterstock

Production Contributors: Teddy Borth, Jennie Forsberg, Grace Hansen

Design Contributors: Candice Keimig, Pakou Moua

Library of Congress Control Number: 2020947670

Publisher's Cataloging-in-Publication Data

Names: Murray, Julie, author.

Title: Western meadowlarks / by Julie Murray

Description: Minneapolis, Minnesota : Abdo Kids, 2022 | Series: State birds | Includes online resources and index.

Identifiers: ISBN 9781098207182 (lib. bdg.) | ISBN 9781098208028 (ebook) | ISBN 9781098208448 (Read-to-Me ebook)

Subjects: LCSH: State birds--Juvenile literature. | Meadowlarks--Juvenile literature. | Birds--Behavior--United States--Juvenile literature.

Classification: DDC 598.297--dc23

Table of Contents

Western Meadowlarks 4

State Bird 22

Glossary 23

Index 24

Abdo Kids Code 24

Western Meadowlarks

Western meadowlarks live in North America.

They like open, grassy areas.

They are mostly brown in color. They have stripes.

Their chests are bright yellow.

The chest has a black V.

Their tails are short.

Their beaks are long and thin.

They eat bugs and seeds.

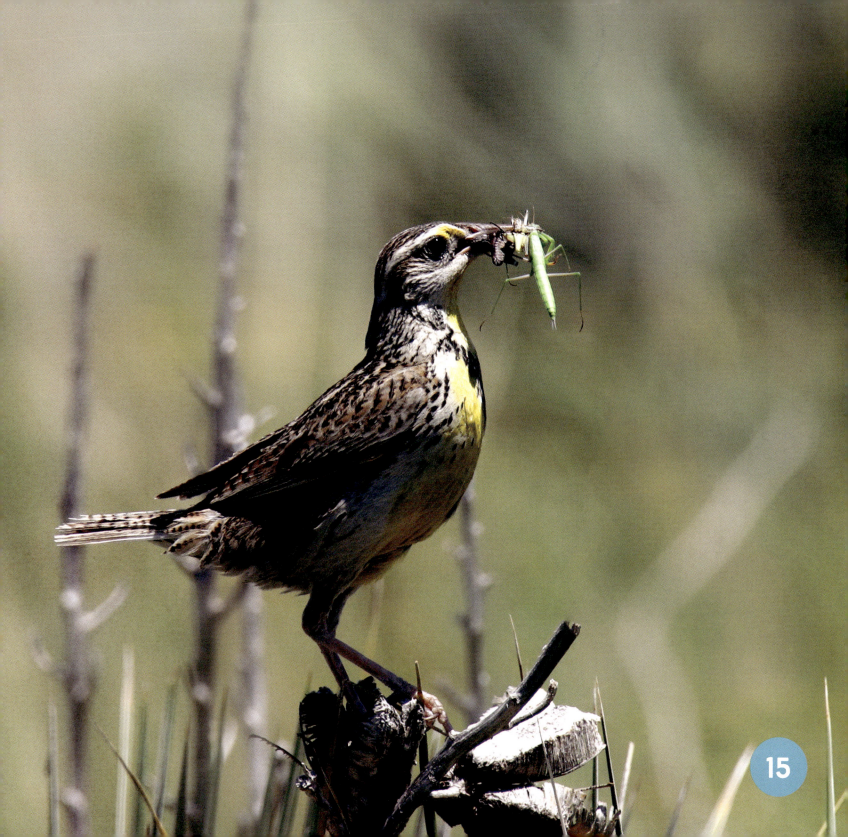

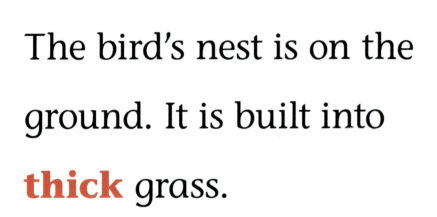

The bird's nest is on the ground. It is built into **thick** grass.

Females lay 3 to 7 eggs.

The eggs are white.

They have brown spots.

The eggs **hatch** in 2 weeks.

The **chicks** will fly soon!

State Bird

KS — Kansas | MT — Montana | NE — Nebraska | ND — North Dakota | OR — Oregon | WY — Wyoming

22

Glossary

chick
a bird that has just hatched or a young bird.

hatch
to come out of an egg.

thick
having many parts that are very close together.

Index

beak 14

chicks 20

color 8, 10, 18

eggs 18, 20

food 14

habitat 6, 16

markings 8, 10, 18

nest 16

North America 4

tail 12

Visit **abdokids.com** to access crafts, games, videos, and more!

Use Abdo Kids code **SWK7182** or scan this QR code!